W9-BSE-950

To:

From:

PETER PAUPER PRESS
Fine Books and Gifts Since 1928

OUR COMPANY

In 1928, at the age of twenty-two, Peter Beilenson began printing books on a small press in the basement of his parents' home in Larchmont, New York. Peter—and later, his wife, Edna—sought to create fine books that sold at "prices even a pauper could afford."

Today, still family owned and operated, Peter Pauper Press continues to honor our founders' legacy—and our customers' expectations—of beauty, quality, and value.

Quotations in this compilation are excerpted from the *Federalist Papers* and from the Papers of Alexander Hamilton collection at founders.archives. gov. Images are sourced from Wikimedia Commons and from the Alexander Hamilton Papers at the New York Public Library.

Designed by
David Cole Wheeler

Visit us at www.peterpauper.com

Alexander
HAMILTON

Wit &
Wisdom

Contents

ALEXANDER HAMILTON,
the writer

*A*merica's first Secretary of the Treasury lived and died by his razor wit. Abandoned by his father and orphaned by the death of his mother, young Hamilton first made waves with his written account of the hurricane that devastated the Caribbean island on which he lived. When a local newspaper published his essay, Hamilton's stirring turn of phrase moved a group of local businessmen to sponsor his education. In late 1772 he left the island of St. Croix for North America, and was well on his way to making history.

Hamilton fell in with young revolutionaries at King's College. He penned eloquent defenses of the revolutionary cause and scathing retorts to British loyalists' arguments. When tensions erupted into war, he joined a volunteer militia, fought in the early battles of the American

Revolution, and served as aide to General
George Washington. At the war-winning
Battle of Yorktown, he led troops to victory
as a commander in his own right.

The Revolutionary War concluded, Hamilton went on to fight many equally fierce
battles of statecraft. President Washington
appointed him Secretary of the Treasury,
and from that position he enacted policies
whose effects resonate to this day. He
defended his positions ferociously, winning friends but also bitter enemies. His
refusal to stray from his principles eventually cost him his political career and, in
what would become America's most famous
duel, his life. He lived by the dictates of his
conscience, and his last letters show that
he was satisfied with the choice—indeed,
that he could have made no other.

On Human Nature

I have thought it my duty to exhibit things as they are, not as they ought to be.

The sacred rights of mankind are not to be rummaged for among old parchments or musty records. They are written, as with a sunbeam, in the whole volume of human nature, by the hand of the divinity itself; and can never be erased or obscured by mortal power.

So numerous indeed and so powerful are the causes which serve to give a false bias to the judgment, that we, upon many occasions, see wise and good men on the wrong as well as on the right side of questions of the first magnitude to society.

Detail of Battle of York Town and gallantry of Hamilton Oct. 1781
from the bronze doors to the Senate wing of the U.S. Capitol

A fondness for power is implanted in most men, and it is natural to abuse it when acquired.

Ambition without principle never was long under the guidance of good sense.

All communities divide themselves into the few and the many.

The best way of determining disputes and of investigating truth, is by descending to elementary principles. Any other method may only bewilder and misguide the understanding.

I never expect to see a perfect work from imperfect man.

Men often oppose a thing, merely because they have had no agency in planning it, or because it may have been planned by those whom they dislike. But if they have been consulted, and have happened to disapprove, opposition then becomes, in their estimation, an indispensable duty of self-love.

The passions of a revolution are apt to hurry even good men into excesses.

That unity is conducive to energy will not be disputed. Decision, activity, secrecy, and dispatch will generally characterise the proceedings of one man, in a much more eminent degree, than the proceedings of any greater number; and in proportion as the number is increased, these qualities will be diminished.

The desire of reward is one of the strongest incentives of human conduct . . .
the best security for the fidelity of mankind is to make their interest coincide with their duty.

An ambitious man too, when he found himself seated on the summit of his country's honors, when he looked forward to the time at which he must descend from the exalted eminence forever, and reflected that no exertion of merit on his part could save him from the unwelcome reverse: Such a man, in such a situation, would be much more violently tempted to embrace a favorable conjuncture for attempting the prolongation of his power, at every personal hazard, than if he had the probability of answering the same end by doing his duty.

When the sword is once drawn, the passions of men observe no bounds of moderation.

Experience is the oracle of truth; and where its responses are unequivocal, they ought to be conclusive and sacred.

Lies often detected and refuted are still revived and repeated, in the hope that the refutation may have been forgotten or that the frequency and boldness of accusation may supply the place of truth and proof.

There are men who could neither be distressed nor won into a sacrifice of their duty; but this stern virtue is the growth of few soils; and in the main it will be found that a power over a man's support is a power over his will.

Justification seldom circulates as rapidly
and as widely as slander.

We seem not to reflect, that in human
society, there is scarcely any plan, however
salutary to the whole and to every part,
by the share, each has in the common
prosperity, but in one way, or another, and
under particular circumstances, will oper-
ate more to the benefit of some parts, than
of others. Unless we can overcome this
narrow disposition and learn to estimate
measures, by their general tendency, we
shall never be a great or a happy people, if
we remain a people at all.

One great error is that we suppose mankind to be more honest than they are.

Men are rather reasoning than reasonable animals for the most part governed by the impulse of passion. This is a truth well understood by our adversaries who have practised upon it with no small benefit to their cause. For at the very moment they are eulogizing the reason of men & professing to appeal only to that faculty, they are courting the strongest & most active passion of the human heart—VANITY!

Experience teaches, that men are often so much governed by what they are accustomed to see and practice, that the simplest and most obvious improvements, in the most ordinary occupations, are adopted with hesitation, reluctance and by slow gradations.

In times of such commotion as the present,
while the passions of men are worked
up to an uncommon pitch there is great
danger of fatal extremes.

Though it cannot be pretended that the
principles of moral and political knowl-
edge have in general the same degree of
certainty with those of the mathematics;
yet they have much better claims in this
respect, than to judge from the conduct of
men in particular situations, we should be
disposed to allow them. The obscurity is
much oftener in the passions and prejudices
of the reasoner than in the subject. Men
upon too many occasions do not give their
own understandings fair play; but yielding
to some untoward bias they entangle
themselves in words and confound themselves in subtleties.

There is a certain enthusiasm in liberty,
that makes human nature rise above itself
in acts of bravery and heroism.

The public mind fatigued at length with
resistance to the calumnies which eternally
assail it, is apt in the end to sit down with
the opinion that a person so often accused
cannot be entirely innocent.

Prejudice and private interest will be
antagonists too powerful for public spirit
and public good.

The authorised maxims and practices of
war are the satire of human nature.

Be virtuous amidst the Seductions of
ambition, and you can hardly in any event
be unhappy.

FEDERALIST;

A COLLECTION

OF

E S S A Y S,

WRITTEN IN FAVOUR OF THE

NEW CONSTITUTION,

AS AGREED UPON BY THE FEDERAL CONVENTION,
SEPTEMBER 17, 1787.

IN TWO VOLUMES.

VOL. I.

NEW-YORK:

PRINTED AND SOLD BY J. AND A. M'LEAN,
No. 41, HANOVER-SQUARE.
M,DCC,LXXXVIII.

Title page of a copy of The Federalist *inscribed from
Elizabeth Hamilton to her sister Angelica Church*

ON GOVERNMENT

Peace made . . . a new scene opens.
The object then will be to make our independence a blessing. To do this we must secure our union on solid foundations; an herculean task and to effect which mountains of prejudice must be levelled!

Why has government been instituted at all? Because the passions of men will not conform to the dictates of reason and justice, without constraint.

In the usual progress of things, the necessities of a nation in every stage of its existence will be found at least equal to its resources.

Civil liberty is only natural liberty, modified and secured by the sanctions of civil society. It is not a thing, in its own nature, precarious and dependent on human will and caprice; but it is conformable to the constitution of man, as well as necessary to the well-being of society.

A sacred respect for the constitutional law is the vital principle, the sustaining energy of a free government.

Is it not time to awake from the deceitful dream of a golden age, and to adopt as a practical maxim for the direction of our political conduct that we, as well as the other inhabitants of the globe, are yet remote from the happy empire of perfect wisdom and perfect virtue?

When human laws contradict or discountenance the means, which are necessary to preserve the essential rights of any society, they defeat the proper end of all laws, and so become null and void.

Civil liberty cannot possibly have any existence, where the society, for whom laws are made, have no share in making them; and where the interest of their legislators is not inseparably interwoven with theirs.

Who can doubt that the happiness of the people . . . would be promoted by competent authorities in the proper hands, to provide the revenues which the necessities of the public might require?

The origin of all civil government, justly established, must be a voluntary compact, between the rulers and the ruled; and must be liable to such limitations, as are necessary for the security of the absolute rights of the latter; for what original title can any man or set of men have, to govern others, except their own consent? To usurp dominion over a people, in their own despite, or to grasp at a more extensive power than they are willing to entrust, is to violate that law of nature, which gives every man a right to his personal liberty; and can, therefore, confer no obligation to obedience.

It is a known fact in human nature that its affections are commonly weak in proportion to the distance or diffusiveness of the object. Upon the same principle that a man is more attached to his family than to his neighbourhood, to his neighbourhood than to the community at large, the people of each State would be apt to feel a stronger bias towards their local governments than towards the government of the Union; unless the force of that principle should be destroyed by a much better administration of the latter.

It is . . . evident to a demonstration, that unless every free agent in America be permitted to enjoy the same privilege, we are entirely stripped of the benefits of the constitution.

Power being almost always the rival of power; the General Government will at all times stand ready to check the usurpations of the state governments; and these will have the same disposition towards the General Government. The people, by throwing themselves into either scale, will infallibly make it preponderate. If their rights are invaded by either, they can make use of the other, as the instrument of redress.

A government continually at a distance and out of sight, can hardly be expected to interest the sensations of the people.

The People of the United States do
ordain and establish this constitution for the government of themselves and their Posterity.

Article I

§1. The Legislative power shall be vested in two
distinct bodies of men one to be called the
Assembly the other the Senate, subject to the
negative hereafter mentioned.

§2. The executive power, with the qualifications
hereafter specified, shall be vested in a
President of the United States.

§3. The Supreme Judicial authority except
in the cases otherwise provided for in the constitution
shall be vested in a court to have cognizance. The
Supreme Court to consist of not less than
six nor more than twelve Judges.

Article II

§1. The Assembly shall consist of persons to be
called representatives who shall be chosen except
in the first instance by the free male citizens
and inhabitants of the several States comprehended
in the Union all of whom of the age of
one year and upwards, shall be entitled to
an equal vote.

Alexander Hamilton's early draft of a constitution for America

Every power vested in a Government is in its nature sovereign, and includes by force of the term, a right to employ all the means requisite, and fairly applicable to the attainment of the ends of such power; and which are not precluded by restrictions and exceptions specified in the constitution, or not immoral, or not contrary to the essential ends of political society.

It seems to have been reserved to the people of this country, by their conduct and example, to decide the important question, whether societies of men are really capable or not, of establishing good government from reflection and choice, or whether they are forever destined to depend, for their political constitutions, on accident and force.

Let us recollect that peace or war will not always be left to our option; that however moderate or unambitious we may be, we cannot count upon the moderation, or hope to extinguish the ambition of others.

To cherish and stimulate the activity of the human mind, by multiplying the objects of enterprise, is not among the least considerable of the expedients, by which the wealth of a nation may be promoted. Even things in themselves not positively advantageous, sometimes become so, by their tendency to provoke exertion. Every new scene, which is opened to the busy nature of man to rouse and exert itself, is the addition of a new energy to the general stock of effort.

Real liberty is neither found in despotism or the extremes of democracy, but in moderate governments.

Cx/

The violent destruction of life and property incident to war, the continual effort and alarm attendant on a state of continual danger, will compel nations the most attached to liberty to resort for repose and security to institutions which have a tendency to destroy their civil and political rights. To be more safe, they at length become willing to run the risk of being less free.

Cx/

Nothing could be more ill-judged than that intolerant spirit which has, at all times, characterized political parties.

If individuals enter into a state of society, the laws of that society must be the supreme regulator of their conduct. If a number of political societies enter into a larger political society, the laws which the latter may enact, pursuant to the powers entrusted to it by its constitution, must necessarily be supreme over those societies, and the individuals of whom they are composed. It would otherwise be a mere treaty, dependent on the good faith of the parties, and not a government; which is only another word for political power and supremacy.

A government ill executed, whatever it may be in theory, must be in practice a bad government.

Our prevailing passions are ambition and interest; and it will ever be the duty of a wise government to avail itself of those passions, in order to make them subservient to the public good—for these ever induce us to action.

Is it not (we may ask these projectors in politics) the true interest of all nations to cultivate the same benevolent and philosophic spirit?

There is, in the nature of sovereign power, an impatience of control, that disposes those who are invested with the exercise of it, to look with an evil eye upon all external attempts to restrain or direct its operations.

In a civil society, it is the duty of each particular branch to promote, not only the good of the whole community, but the good of every other particular branch: If one part endeavours to violate the rights of another, the rest ought to assist in preventing the injury: When they do not, but remain neutral, they are deficient in their duty, and may be regarded, in some measure, as accomplices.

To look for a continuation of harmony between a number of independent unconnected sovereignties, situated in the same neighbourhood, would be to disregard the uniform course of human events, and to set at defiance the accumulated experience of ages.

The safety of the whole depends upon the mutual protection of every part. If the sword of oppression be permitted to lop off one limb without opposition, reiterated strokes will soon dismember the whole body.

In popular governments 'tis useful that those who propose measures should partake in whatever dangers they may involve.

The design of civil society . . . is that the united strength of the several members might give stability and security to the whole body, and each respective member; so that one part cannot encroach upon another, without becoming a common enemy, and eventually endangering the safety and happiness of all the other parts.

The representative . . . is bound by every possible tie to consult the advantage of his constituent. Gratitude for the high and honourable trust reposed in him demands a return of attention and regard to the advancement of his happiness. Self-interest, that most powerful incentive of human actions, points and attracts towards the same object.

The duration of his trust is not perpetual; but must expire in a few years, and if he is desirous of the future favour of his constituents, he must not abuse the present instance of it; but must pursue the end, for which he enjoys it; otherwise he forfeits it, and defeats his own purpose.

Justice is the end of government. It is the end of civil society. It ever has been, and ever will be, pursued, until it be obtained, or until liberty be lost in the pursuit. In a society, under the forms of which the stronger faction can readily unite and oppress the weaker, anarchy may as truly be said to reign, as in a state of nature where the weaker individual is not secured against the violence of the stronger: And as in the latter state even the stronger individuals are prompted by the uncertainty of their condition, to submit to a government which may protect the weak, as well as themselves: so in the former state, will the more powerful factions be gradually induced by a like motive, to wish for a government which will protect all parties, the weaker as well as the more powerful.

If the federal government should overpass the just bounds of its authority and make a tyrannical use of its powers, the people, whose creature it is, must appeal to the standard they have formed, and take such measures to redress the injury done to the Constitution as the exigency may suggest and prudence justify.

In politics, as in religion, it is equally absurd to aim at making proselytes by fire and sword. Heresies in either can rarely be cured by persecution.

It may be truly said of every government, as well as of that of the United States, that it has only a right, to pass such laws as are necessary and proper to accomplish the objects intrusted to it. For no government has a right to do merely what it pleases.

All governments, even the most despotic, depend, in a great degree, on opinion. In free republics, it is most peculiarly the case: In these, the will of the people makes the essential principle of the government; and the laws which control the community, receive their tone and spirit from the public wishes.

A council to a magistrate, who is himself responsible for what he does, are generally nothing better than a clog upon his good intentions, are often the instruments and accomplices of his bad and are almost always a cloak to his faults.

The history of human conduct does not warrant that exalted opinion of human virtue which would make it wise in a nation to commit interests of so delicate and momentous a kind as those which concern its intercourse with the rest of the world to the sole disposal of a magistrate, created and circumstanced, as would be a President of the United States.

The complete independence of the Courts of justice is peculiarly essential in a limited Constitution. By a limited Constitution, I understand one which contains certain specified exceptions to the Legislative authority; such, for instance, as that it shall pass no bills of attainder, no ex post facto laws, and the like. Limitations of this kind can be preserved in practice no other way than through the medium of the Courts of justice; whose duty it must be to declare all Acts contrary to the manifest tenor of the Constitution void. Without this, all the reservations of particular rights or privileges would amount to nothing.

Has it been found that bodies of men act with more rectitude or greater disinterestedness than individuals? The contrary of this has been inferred by all accurate observers of the conduct of mankind; and the inference is founded upon obvious reasons. Regard to reputation has a less active influence, when the infamy of a bad action is to be divided among a number than when it is to fall singly upon one. A spirit of faction, which is apt to mingle its poison in the deliberations of all bodies of men, will often hurry the persons of whom they are composed into improprieties and excesses, for which they would blush in a private capacity.

If the legislature can disfranchise any number of citizens at pleasure by general descriptions, it may soon confine all the votes to a small number of partizans, and establish an aristocracy or an oligarchy; if it may banish at discretion all those whom particular circumstances render obnoxious, without hearing or trial, no man can be safe, nor know when he may be the innocent victim of a prevailing faction. The name of liberty applied to such a government would be a mockery of common sense.

There can be no truer principle than this— that every individual of the community at large has an equal right to the protection of government.

Government implies the power of making laws. It is essential to the idea of a law, that it be attended with a sanction; or, in other words, a penalty or punishment for disobedience.

The fabric of American Empire ought to rest on the solid basis of THE CONSENT OF THE PEOPLE. The streams of national power ought to flow immediately from that pure original fountain of all legitimate authority.

The system, though it may not be perfect in every part, is, upon the whole, a good one; is the best that the present views and circumstances of the country will permit; and is such an one as promises every species of security which a reasonable people can desire.

Neither the suggestion of pride nor timidity ought to guide. There ought to be much cool calculation united with much calm fortitude. The Government ought to be all intellect while the people ought to be all feeling.

It is evidently of the greatest moment that the people should be united and circumspect; and that their rulers should be men who will neither be seduced by interest, nor impelled by passion into designs or measures, which may justly forfeit the confidence or friendship of the other members of the great national society.

All men have one common original: they
participate in one common nature, and
consequently have one common right.
No reason can be assigned why one man
should exercise any power, or pre-
eminence over his fellow creatures more
than another; unless they have voluntarily
vested him with it.

The parliament claims a right to tax us in
all cases whatsoever: Its late acts are in
virtue of that claim. How ridiculous then is
it to affirm, that we are quarrelling for the
trifling sum of three pence a pound on tea;
when it is evidently the principle against
which we contend.

When the political salvation of any community is depending, it is incumbent upon those who are set up as its guardians, to embrace such measures, as have justice, vigour, and a probability of success to recommend them.

A government ought to contain in itself every power requisite to the full accomplishment of the objects committed to its care, and to the complete execution of the trusts for which it is responsible; free from every other control, but a regard to the public good and to the sense of the people.

We have now happily concluded the great work of independence, but much remains to be done to reach the fruits of it.

The spirit of enterprise, useful and prolific as it is, must necessarily be contracted or expanded in proportion to the simplicity or variety of the occupations and productions, which are to be found in a Society.

The idea of an actual representation of all classes of the people by persons of each class is altogether visionary.

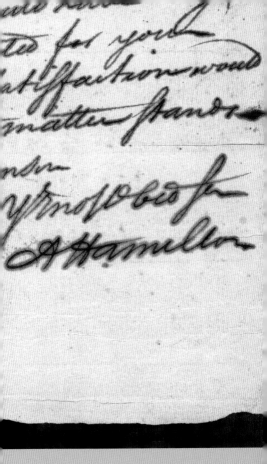

Excerpt from a letter written by Alexander Hamilton in 1778

ALEXANDER HAMILTON,
the man

While Hamilton's pen made him powerful
enemies, it also forged the connections that
sustained him throughout his life. Hamilton's letters and other writings reveal the
person behind the firebrand—the life he
lived in private while working toward his
vision of the public good. His impassioned
attachment to his principles can be seen
equally in his attachments to his friends—
from ally Marquis de Lafayette, to fellow
revolutionary John Laurens, to dryly witty
sister-in-law Angelica Church—and to his
beloved wife, Elizabeth.

Hamilton's scorn was as withering as his
affection was moving. Whether poking
gentle fun or assailing a political rival's
character, his verbal barbs stuck in many a
memory and a craw. His political adversaries included John Adams (whose reelection
Hamilton arguably scuppered with a

defamatory pamphlet), Thomas Jefferson, and former friend James Madison. One such rivalry was ultimately his undoing.

In the 1804 election for the governor of New York, Hamilton supported Morgan Lewis instead of Aaron Burr, who he felt was unfit for the position. Hamilton's opposition had already more or less cost Burr a presidential election, and Burr was incensed. The two exchanged a series of angry letters (Burr's full of outrage, Hamilton's full of sly jabs), culminating in a duel. On July 11, 1804, Hamilton faced Burr and, instead of shooting at his opponent, discharged his pistol into the air. Burr mortally wounded Hamilton.

It was the end of Hamilton's life but not his legacy.

ON LIFE

A garden, you know, is a very usual refuge of a disappointed politician. Accordingly, I have purchased a few acres about nine miles from town, have built a house, and am cultivating a garden.

For one cannot always live on hope. 'Tis thin diet at best.

Real firmness is good for anything; strut is good for nothing.

Photo of Hamilton Grange, New York, NY, where Hamilton lived the last two years of his life

If truly this be, as every appearance indicates, a conspiracy of vice against virtue, ought I not rather to be flattered, that I have been so long and so peculiarly an object of persecution?

❧

. . . but as he is an honest fellow, I shall be glad he may find some employment, that will enable him to get knocked in the head in an honorable way.

❧

His sedentary exploits are sung in strains of laborious dulness. The many breeches he has worn out during the war are enumerated, nor are the depredations which long sitting has made on his _____ unsung.

I cannot be the apologist of any vice because the ardour of passion may have made it mine.

I feel that nothing can ever compensate for the loss of the enjoyments I leave at home, or can ever put my heart at tolerable ease. In the bosom of my family alone must my happiness be sought.

And what is there can be put in competition with the sweet affections of the heart?

To indulge these the more freely is with me a principal motive for relinquishing an office in which 'tis said I have gained some glory and the difficulties of which had just been subdued.

From wartime letters to
ELIZABETH HAMILTON:

I remonstrate with my heart on the impropriety of suffering itself to be engrossed by an individual of the human race when so many millions ought to participate in its affections and in its cares. But it constantly presents you under such amiable forms as seem too well to justify its meditated desertion of the cause of country, humanity, and of glory I would say, if there were not something in the sound insipid and ridiculous when compared with the sacrifices by which it is to be attained.

How chequered is human life! How precarious is happiness! How easily do we often part with it for a shadow! These are the reflections that frequently intrude themselves upon me, with a painful application. I am going to do my duty.

Alexander Hamilton (1757-1804) in the Uniform
of the New York Artillery *by Alonzo Chappel*

From a letter to
JOHN LAURENS:

You know the opinion I entertain of
mankind, and how much it is my desire
to preserve myself free from particular
attachments, and to keep my happiness
independent on the caprice of others.
You should not have taken advantage of
my sensibility to steal into my affections
without my consent. But as you have
done it and as we are generally indulgent
to those we love, I shall not scruple to
pardon the fraud you have committed, on
condition that for my sake, if not for your
own, you will always continue to merit
the partiality, which you have so artfully
instilled into me.

Portrait of John Laurens by Charles Wilson Peale, 1780

From letters to
ANGELICA SCHUYLER CHURCH:

Amiable Angelica! How much you are
formed to endear yourself to every good
heart! How deeply you have rooted yourself in the affections of your friends on this
side the Atlantic! Some of us are and must
continue inconsolable for your absence.

❧

You are always of more consequence than
the great affairs which you have so often
represented as the rival of all my friend
ships.

❧

If you knew the power you have to make
happy You would lose no opportunity of
writing to Betsey & me; for we literally
feast on your letters. . . . Life is too short to
warrant procrastination of the most favourite
and precious objects.

*Portrait of Angelica Church, her son, and a servant
by John Trumbull, 1780*

From a letter to AARON BURR, *preceding their duel:*

I deem it inadmissible, on principle,
to consent to be interrogated as to the
justness of the inferences, which may be
drawn by others, from whatever I may
have said of a political opponent in the
course of a fifteen years competition.

I stand ready to avow or disavow promptly
and explicitly any precise or definite
opinion, which I may be charged with
having declared of any Gentleman. More
than this cannot fitly be expected from me.

Between Gentlemen, despicable and more
despicable are not worth the pains of a
distinction.

I trust, on more reflection, you will see the
matter in the same light with me. If not, I
can only regret the circumstance, and must
abide the consequences.

The duel between Alexander Hamilton and Aaron Burr,
from a painting by J. Mund

From Hamilton's statement of intent before the duel:

I have resolved, if our interview is con-
ducted in the usual manner, and it pleases
God to give me the opportunity, to reserve
and throw away my first fire . . .

From Hamilton's parting letter to ELIZABETH HAMILTON:

I need not tell you of the pangs I feel, from
the idea of quitting you and exposing you
to the anguish which I know you would
feel. Nor could I dwell on the topic lest it
should unman me. . . . With my last idea;
I shall cherish the sweet hope of meeting
you in a better world. Adieu best of wives
and best of Women.

Portrait of Elizabeth Hamilton by Ralph Earl, c. 1787

From the eulogy for
ALEXANDER HAMILTON
delivered by
Gouverneur Morris:

I charge you to protect his fame—It is all he has left—all that these poor orphan children will inherit from their father. But, my countrymen, that Fame may be a rich treasure to you also. Let it be the test by which to examine those who solicit your favour. Disregarding professions, view their conduct and on a doubtful occasion, ask, Would Hamilton have done this thing?